SCHOOL PSYCHOLOGIST COLORING BOOK

KEEP TALKING

I'M DIAGNOSING YOU

Published by Ashokabuddha Tripathi Publishing

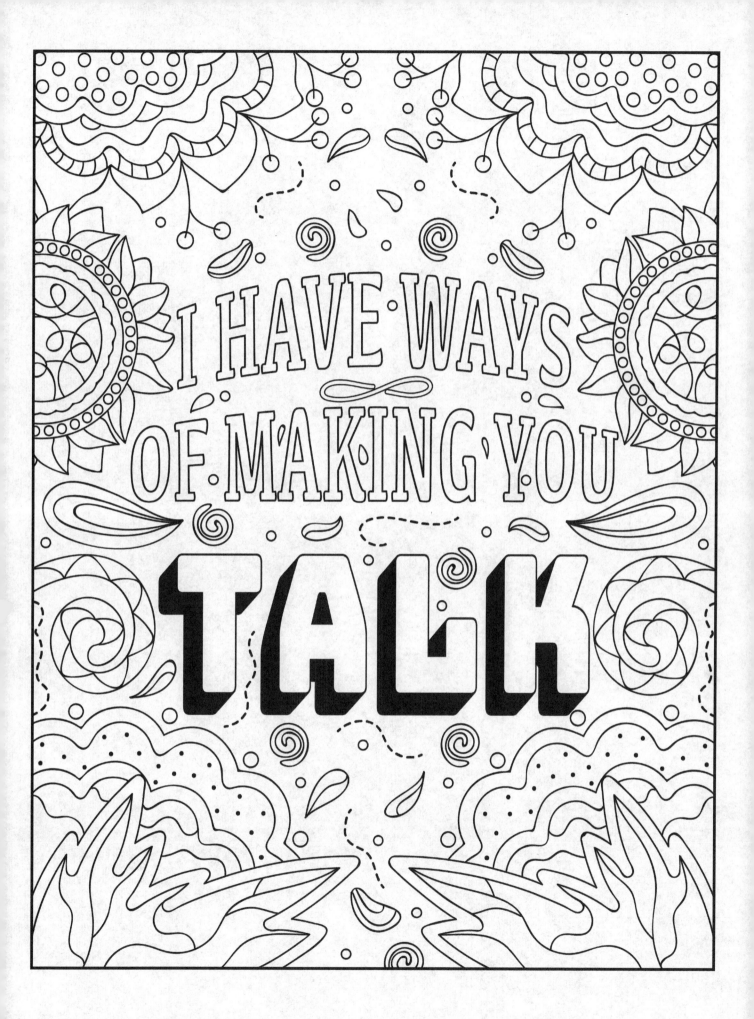

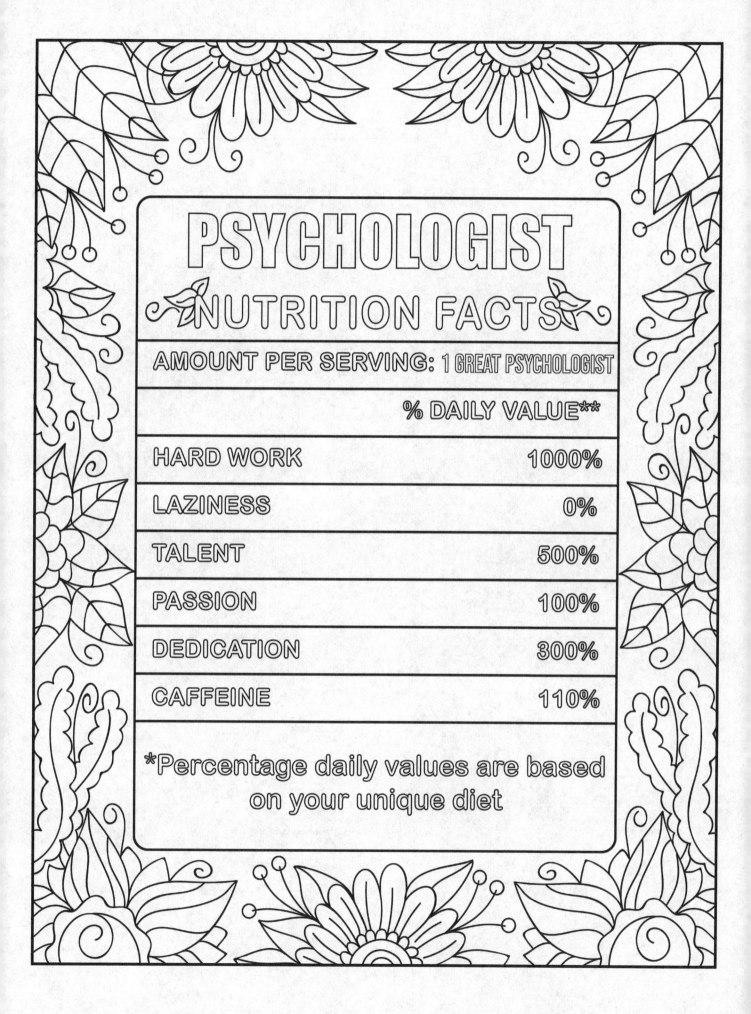

PSYCHOLOGIST
NUTRITION FACTS

AMOUNT PER SERVING: 1 GREAT PSYCHOLOGIST

% DAILY VALUE**

HARD WORK	1000%
LAZINESS	0%
TALENT	500%
PASSION	100%
DEDICATION	300%
CAFFEINE	110%

*Percentage daily values are based on your unique diet

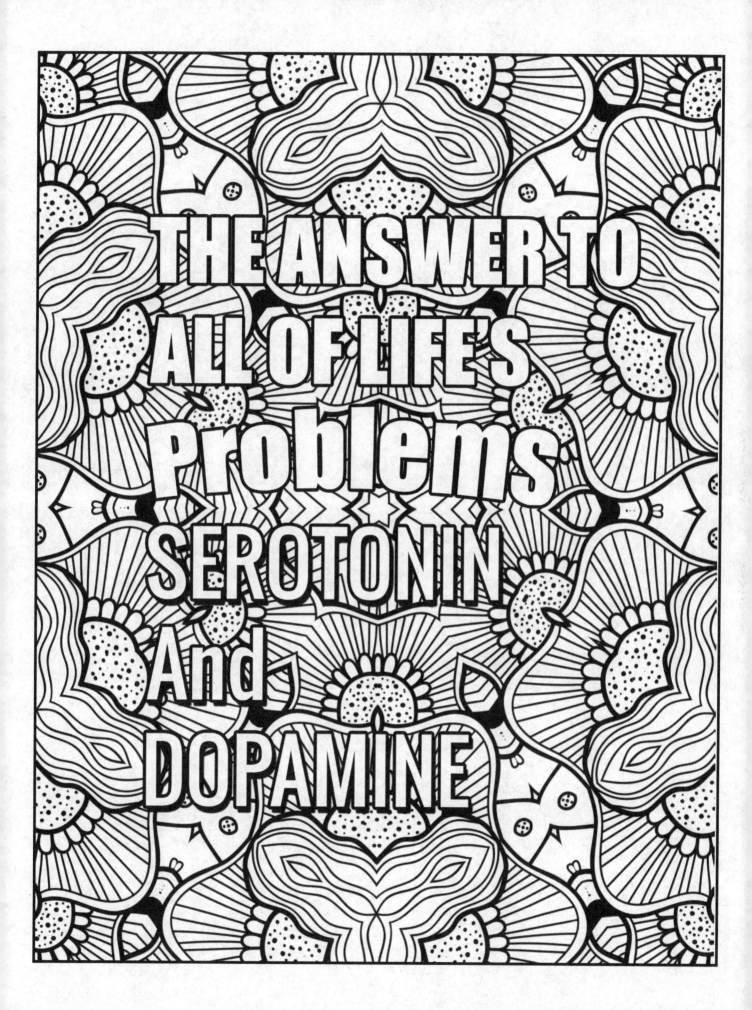

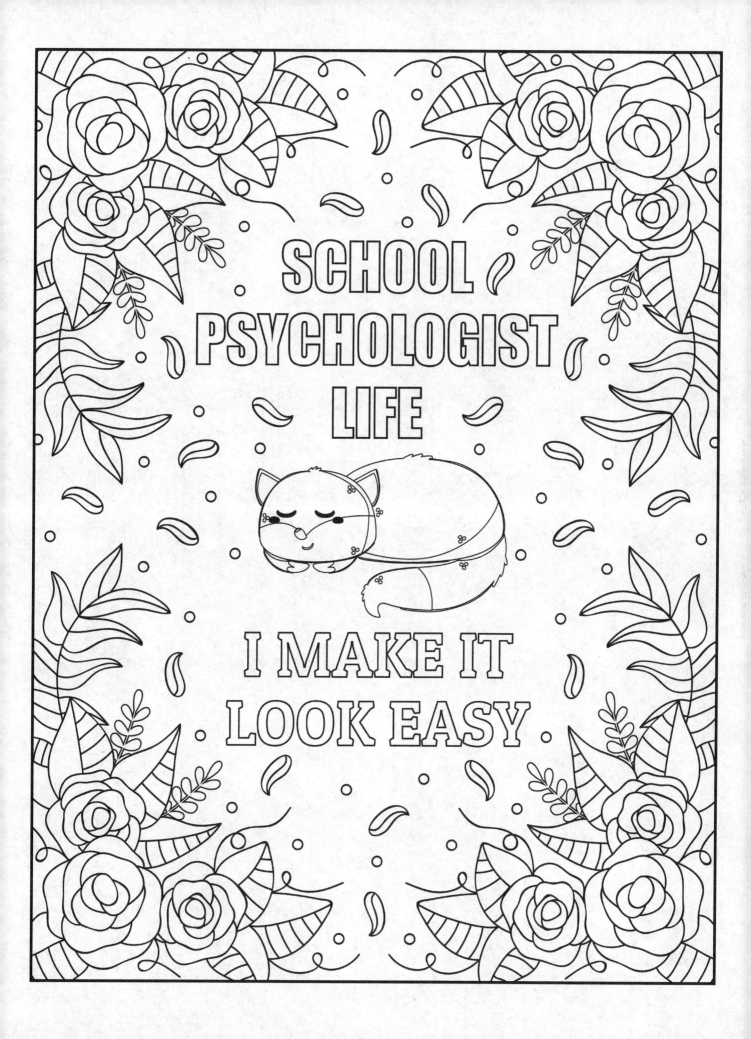

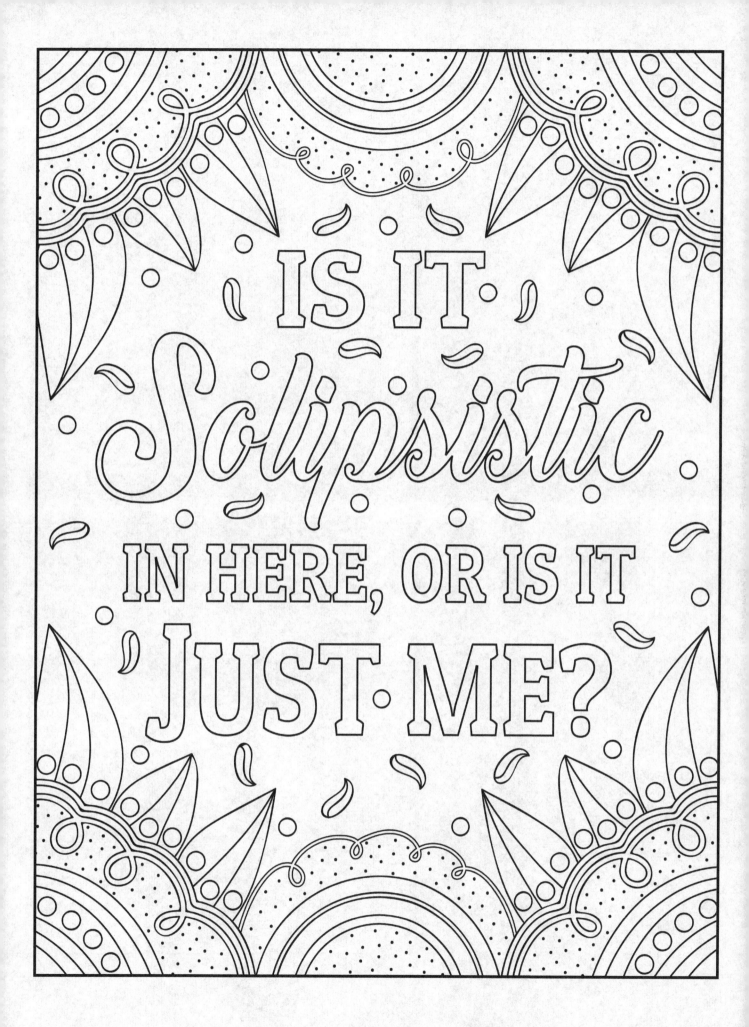

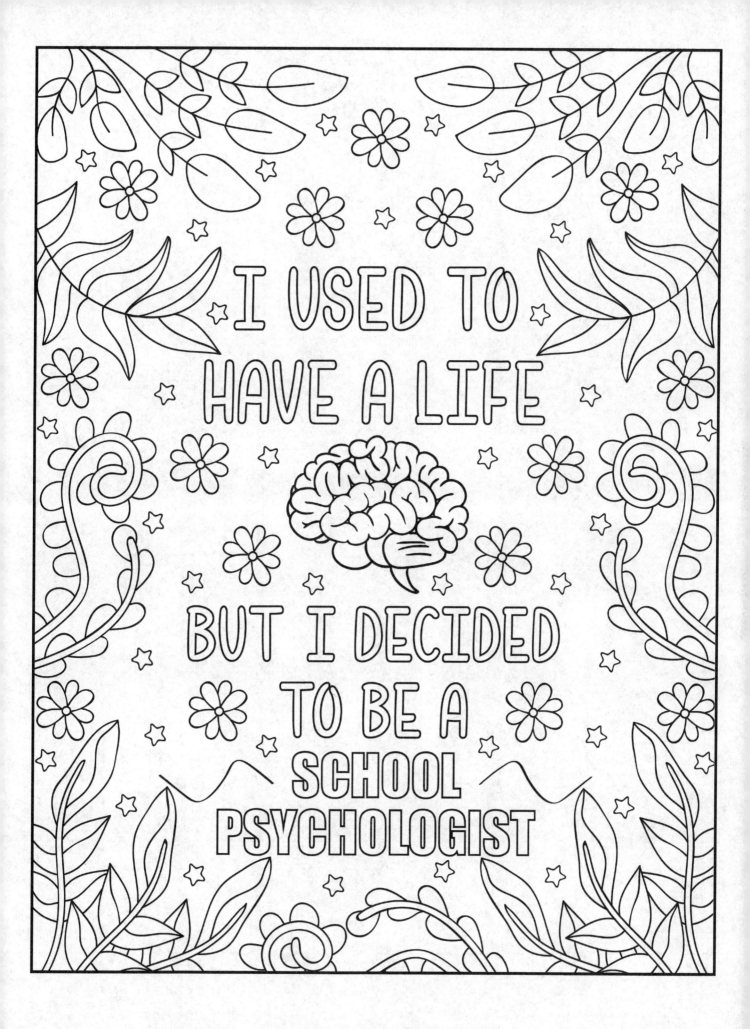

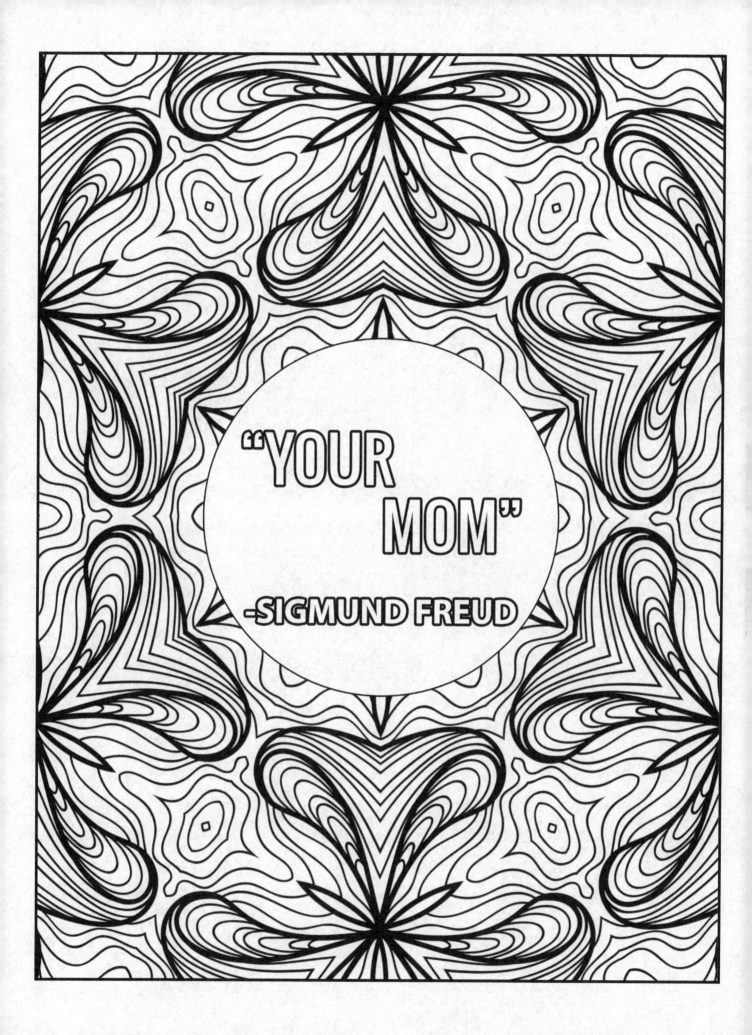

Made in United States
Troutdale, OR
01/04/2025

27612593R00031